To My Inner Child

By Alexa Suarez V.

DISCLAIMER

This book may touch sensitive topics that may be triggering.

This is to all of those who live through the eyes of their inner child.

To my younger siblings, I hope that I gave your inner child time to grow.

-Alexa S.V

Table Of Contents

To My Inner Child

To my inner child,

Who grew up so fast,

Too fast that by the age of eight you held more
responsibilities

Than you could handle.

Heaven knows how hard I have fought and tried to
save you

From the clutches of the monsters that walked

In the daylight.

Despite the time that has flown past your eyes,

I take you with me,

So you can finally do the things you couldn't.

All I Can Say Is...

I'm sorry you had to grow up so fast.

Repercussions

I wish I could've protected you sooner.

Then maybe, you would've been happier,

And I would've been less broken.

Release

It's okay to let go of people who have hurt you.

Of course, whenever you're ready.

No Mistakes

How quickly chalks turn into markers,

markers into pencils

and pencils into pens.

With chalk marks—those can be washed away.

Marker stains can be cleaned.

And pencil marks

can be erased.

As adults, pens are used

Because we have learned that with pens

Those marks become as permanent as our actions.

Like a signature signed on fine paper.

While some were given chalks as kids,

Those in similar positions as I,

Only have known pens.

What Could it be ?

Her mind always seemed crowded with worries.

The way her eyebrows furrowed with concern as she stood there by the window looking from the inside.

She was simply a child, with the responsibilities of an adult.

Heaven knows what is going on in that head of hers.

Pennies into gold

Although you didn't have much,

Your imagination

Is what made dirt into glitter

And clouds into cotton candy.

Possibility

Maybe if we lived in another world,

And in another life,

You would smile a bit longer

And have less to lose.

The Difference

The old me wanted to forgive you.

The new me wouldn't give you a second chance.

Words Unspoken

Your eyes tell,

And I read them.

Where did my princess go

?

Little princess don't you cry,

For when you're a queen those girls cannot hurt you.

Their words will mean nothing, and you will stand tall.

My! Oh my! Little princess how much you have grown!

Your gown is as long as your hair

And your crown matches your grace!

Now, don't cry.

Do not let those girls mock you! In fact,

As queen, they shall not matter to you anymore!

My queen,

Do not listen to them,

For their words hold nothing but malice.

Turn your head and do not let them know you are bothered.

My queen, are you okay?

I see red in your eyes.

Do not let them let you turn sour.

Surely, they will meet their own ends on their own.

My queen,

You have aged over the years.

I didn't realize it at first, but your demeanor has changed.

You have silenced them indeed, but at the cost of your morals.

Please come back, my little princess...

This is not you.

Come,

Let's have some tea like we use to,

Maybe then you may change your mind and not have blood on your hands.

My queen, what have you done?

Scars that never healed

Nothing hurts more

Then reopened wounds.

Ghostly Friends

I remember the days when I sat on the swings.

There was a little girl whose age was the same as mine.

Like me, she was alone.

We swung side by side for what felt like hours.

She would talk and I would listen.

She wore a blue puffy polka dot dress,

Pearls around her neck,

And had the uttermost blond hair I've ever seen.

On the days she was gone,

A boy would take her place and sit beside me.

He was kind, gentle, and sweet.

His hair was a nice chestnut brown and appeared to be taller than mine.

Both never were there at the same time at the swings.

Though that did not bother me.

Despite the concerns of their unspoken tales of their deaths,

All I ever cared about was their company.

I may have not remembered their names.

What I do remember is,

that they made me feel less alone.

There is No Prince

Charming

Sitting there by the window,

One can't help but wonder where he went.

Or if he was coming at all.

Where was sword fighting?

The righteous steed?

The battle to the death and happily ever after?

He was not here to fight off the dragon of the castle.

He was nowhere in sight!

It was ridiculous!

So much so, that I took matters into my own hands.

In fact,

It was I who had built a ladder and who left the tower.

It was I who watched the dragon burn it into flames.

It was I who commanded the dragon instead of slaying it.

After all that waiting, we finally left.

The prince was too late by the time he showed up.

I do not care anymore.

I now have a new home,

And a new pet,

That I can call mine.

You did just Fine

I hope I made you proud.

Because I know I am

Proud of you.

Somehow you still Shined

Those kids were brutal to you.

You saw death in front of your eyes.

Had your clothes, ripped, stepped, and tossed like garbage.

You shed thousands of tears.

Prayed thousands of times.

Lived through your nightmares.

You dealt with it all.

I don't know how you did it,

I really don't.

Even more so,

All while still having a smile on your face.

Unceasing

Despite our age,

I still treasure my stuffed animals as if they lived,

Giggle at the simplest jokes,

Believe in ghosts,

Search for fairies in my garden,

And wait for the day magic flourishes in the palms
of hands.

I refuse to let them.

Let

Them

Kill

our

Spirit.

Anti-Hero

Don't worry.

We became the hero you always needed,

Instead of the villain, they tried to make you out to be.

Though, our blood is now colder.

Internalized Misogyny

For the longest time, I wished I wasn't a girl.

I hated how they treated me differently as

My younger brother

And how he was able to do so much more than
what I can do only because of our gender.

I hate it even more that he doesn't see the problem.

How he thinks that I can do

What he can do,

But not without the consequence of getting
disciplined.

It sucked.

I hate myself so much that I couldn't look in the
mirror.

This occurred for many years until one day,

I found a role model that was more than one of
those delicate princesses.

She was a fighter who wasn't afraid to be herself.

I wanted to be like her.

So I became her.

Even if it meant,

Them hating me.

I am Big Now

You cannot tell me what to wear,

Act,

Or

Speak.

Because I am now me.

I get to choose.

I get to speak.

I get to scream.

Perspective

They say that after it rains,

There is a rainbow.

But that didn't mean a thing,

When everything looks black and white.

Caution

Pardon me,

For being so

Defensive

In a world full of

Guns and knives.

No More Fear

You are safe with me

little one.

You don't have to hide anymore.

You don't need to run

Until your legs bruise.

You don't need to fear the ugly lies

They had put into your head.

I've taken care of each and every

Demon that emerges through the dark clouds

Of your mind.

Here hold my hand and I will guide you,

To a place where we finally belong.

Disclaimer for the pain

There is going to be so much heartbreak

You'll have to face,

To get to

Today.

It's cruel

And

Sadly true.

Sleep Tight

Shush little child,

Go to bed.

The little monsters are just in your head.

Shush little child,

Don't you see?

It's all imaginary.

Shush little child,

Close your eyes.

Soon after you sleep, the sun will rise.

Potential Upbringing

We have come thus far.

With how little we had.

Maybe now,

We'll play games,

That we couldn't before.

Hypocrisy

Looking back,

I realized that you never kept secrets.

We were told by those older than us that it was bad.

So we became an open book.

The most ironic part of it all was that although we didn't keep any personal secrets,

Instead, we held the secrets that other people told us not to tell.

Because apparently,

That was not bad.

Picture Perfect

As a child,

I was told I was average.

My eyes were the average brown.

My hair was average.

My personality was average.

They told me I was nothing special.

I believed them,

Until I stopped caring.

They grew upset at my vibrant personality,

Trying to silence my voice,

And tried to force me into a box filled with
normalcy.

I am not average,

But more so,

I am me.

Finally.

Dull

There is something so

Daunting

About being colorful

In a world that

Shames you for it.

Somewhere I Belong

I dream of a place where I am free.

Somewhere I can fly and touch the sky.

Not neverland nor wonderland

But a mix between the two.

I want to be wild and free.

Without anyone judging me.

A place of imperfections.

Full of random activities.

A place where dreams come true.

Where pixies fly around all day.

Like a bird free from a cage.

A location where there's no worries.

Everyone there is carefree.

They dance like there's no tomorrow.

A place I can call home.

Leaving all the negativity behind.

Somewhere I belong.

A Brutally Honest Truth

I've said,

"I wished

I wasn't born."

Far too many times.

I took the Blame

"Why did you do that?"

~~I didn't.~~

'You're such a liar."

~~I was telling the truth.~~

"Miss, it was her."

~~No it was not.~~

"What a snitch."

~~I didn't say a word.~~

44

"It was you, wasn't it?"

~~No. It was never me.~~

"She did it!"

~~You were the one who told me to do it. You said, it was your fault.~~

"She told me."

~~My lips were sealed.~~

"Alexa, who did it ?"

Me.

Yes, it was me.

45

Responsibilities

I always found it strange

That my peers wanted to grow up so

Quickly.

When that's all that I knew.

It was not fun.

Instead of playing in the streets,

I had babysitting.

Instead of watching Tv shows

Late at night,

I had homework.

While my siblings folded

Paper airplanes,

I folded the laundry.

I still wonder, "What am I missing ?"

Crush or Be Crushed

I've never believed someone could have a crush on
me.

The number of notes I've gotten only to be laughed
at for believing it was true

Or how they did it to mess with my feelings,

It shaped my perception of a crush.

It was always followed up with a "just kidding" or

someone else spreading lies about someone's
affection.

So when I had been confessed to,

I denied them every single time.

Cause I knew there had been a high potential,

Of false feelings followed by

The decline of my self-esteem.

So for those who indeed had a crush on me,

When I didn't believe them.

Just know it wasn't you,

But rather me,

Who was too protective to be fooled.

XOXO

The Curse of the Oldest

All eyes on me.

I was their lab rat.

The second parent.

The babysitter.

So many times

I

Wanted to know what it's like to

Have someone

Older.

So

That

I didn't have to

Take care of

Anyone.

So

That

I

Didn't have to think about

Anyone

But

Myself.

So that maybe I

Didn't always have to

Share.

Maybe

51

My childhood,

And ability to

Be

"Normal"

Wasn't traded

Away.

Holding onto the Sands of Youth

You were always scared.

Scared of growing up.

Even now you had every right to be.

Maybe that is why we still read fantasy books

And

Watch cartoons.

Because we are holding onto

What is left of our adolescence

That slips

Through our

Fingers.

Stopping the Cycle

The younger ones

Never understood why

I was so protective

And why I always

Checked up on them.

I pray,

They may never know.

Instinct

Being the oldest,

It was never a choice,

But rather,

An act of self-enlisted

Duty.

Good Enough

At the age of five,

I had set the bar.

I was the prodigy.

I had to be the brightest bulb,

The fastest runner,

The quickest learner,

And

The overachiever.

When I wasn't

All I could be is

A

Disappointment.

Teacher of all, but never a student

Although the fairy had a pair of

Wings,

She couldn't fly.

No, she could.

She could fly so far away.

Yes, could.

But she wouldn't

No,

Not when she was the only one

To teach others how to fly.

So she stayed and taught

For years and years

With every one of her students to fly.

As she watched them leave

And saw the newcomers come,

Her heart grew envious and distraught.

For whom would ever

Want to take her place?

Therapy Session

Tell me how on earth

Did I end up being

My own therapist?

Concealed

~~They'll never know~~

~~How much weight~~

~~These hands carried.~~

Reinvented

There was a moment

When a child grew tired of

Clichés

And rewrite them

Into something new

because their childhood

wasn't as magical,

and they needed

something more realistic.

Educators

Some teachers are wonderful,

While others seemed like

They needed a career change.

They may think that children

Do not know the difference

As to who made the classroom

A home and who didn't.

Little do they know,

Children do.

Trauma

I wish I were able to

Tell you that

What they did and said to me

Didn't still affect us,

But I would be

Lying straight through

My teeth if I

Did.

How do I recover?

What do you do

With a scraped knee?

You put a band-aid.

What do you do

With an untied shoelace?

You retie it.

Both are arguably easy fixes.

Now,

What do you do

With

Trauma?

Conditional Approval

It's no wonder

Why she was always

quiet.

They praised her for her silence

and punished

her for using her voice.

They are to Blame

There are days when I'm upset,

No,

Not upset,

Angry.

Angry at how they hurt you

Dear child.

You were only a kid.

WE were only a kid.

No Good Deed

What's frustrating

Is seeing the people

Who had bullied,

Hurt,

and harmed

You as a child

Get to move on with their lives.

While you are still healing

From the scars they gave

You.

Throwing Punches

They said, "Just ignore them",

I don't do that *anymore.*

Oh no, I became so much more worse with

vengeance.

They said "go to the adults"

But that only made

Things *worse.*

So I handled them.

Let me ask one thing,

If the hero can fight against

The villains,

Then why am I the one in handcuffs?

Don't drop them

The Juggler was young when he started.

At first, it began with

One ball,

Then two,

Two became three,

And three became six.

One day

While the juggler did a performance,

A ball fell.

He was ruined.

Done for.

He was fired that day.

Sounds Outside

Blankets felt like

The strongest

Shields.

Though they never blocked

Out the

Nightmares

And

The noises

Of arguments.

Too young for this

Such big thoughts

For someone

Who just learned

Their ABC's.

Behind the costumes

Halloween is the season to be anyone,

Interesting enough,

So many choose to dress up as monsters.

Using it to vandalize houses

And chase children.

~~Speaks volumes, doesn't it?~~

Temporarily Free

There was always

Something so liberating

About going on

The swings.

It was the sensation of

Flying when you're at the peak.

But like most things,

There is a stop at the end

As your feet hit the ground.

Flashback

Looking back on the past,

Things slowly became blurry.

Maybe because I

Started blocking it out

Over the years.

Or maybe,

It just wasn't worth the tears anymore.

Out of Place

When everyone talks about what is wrong with
you,

It feels almost like you don't belong.

As if you were an alien from outer space,

Or a hybrid of some kind that is too

Much of one or the other to truly fit in any niche.

It gets lonely.

Tiring.

And most of all suffocating

Smile for the Picture

While one could hide behind a mask.

I hid behind

Smiles

And bright hair bows.

Those frilly dresses

Looked light but

Were heavy as her burdens.

The shoes on her feet felt like thorns.

It was incredibly overbearing yet,

It had to be perfect.

Too perfect

So that it hid all what was underneath it all.

Underlying Magic Beyond Writing

I'll be honest to say,

Although our penmanship is

Terrible,

So many beautiful sentences were written with it.

The Creepy Shed

At my aunt's house that

I had spent my younger days at,

There was this small wooden shed in the backyard.

In that shed, multiple toys stared at the window,
which I use to peer through.

It was always dark as there was no light in the shed.

As a kid, I ~~use to~~ think it was haunted.

I still do.

Muted

It never mattered how much she had screamed or
shouted

In times when all she needed was a hug

No one ever listened anyway.

Engraved in my Brain

The first time I

Got bullied is still unforgettable

And so were

The other times after that.

How my Phobia was Made

I used to not be afraid of restrooms

But I was afraid of the dark.

In my early days of elementary school.

I had three accidents.

Each time I became teased by my fellow third graders.

These accidents happened because I was never shown the restroom or because they had been locked.

One day as I entered the restroom stall.

The door was shut, and the lights were turned off.

After washing my hands I pulled the door with all my might.

It wouldn't budge.

I was too panicked to turn on the lights.

The walls felt like there were closing in each time I pulled the handle.

Now I have claustrophobia and fear that it will happen all over again.

I'm Begging

Please don't make me grow up any faster.

What They Called Me

It was never my name.

It was always

four eyes,

nerd,

boring,

Little miss goody two shoes,

Gullible,

And so much more.

I still remember each and every one they gave me
and who gave me them.

I wouldn't let them get to me, so I owned each and
every one of them.

No matter how much I've grown,

Those names still feel bonded to me

Whether I like it or not.

Not a Child Anymore

I had to tell them

That I killed you.

For them to take us seriously.

Cloud Reader

While looking up in the clouds,

I imagined them almost animated.

Such as how a cloud looked like a dragon,

It would move with its wings and

I was in a car moving away from it.

In a way,

I told many stories

Because of what I saw in the clouds.

Child at Heart

The day I stop yearning for a fictional life is when,

I cannot use my eyes to read,

My ears to listen to stories,

And

My imagination to create fake scenarios.

~

Even when I'm F feet under the ground,

I can assure you that my soul

And myself in the great beyond,

Will still somewhere and somehow

Continue to dream.

Who's Laughing Now ?

There were days at school,

Where I was mocked,

Laughed,

And

Bullied for

My magical childish nature.

What they don't know.

Is that now.

I use my imagination

To my advantage.

Losing the Magic

It's quite sad

How as we grow older,

Some have lost the light in their eyes,

Simply because they are told to grow up

A little too soon.

Never at One Place

Moving every other year was exhausting.

A new set of faces with every single school I attended.

I'm not sure if it was the schools or the people who attended,

But the same would happen.

New playgrounds and new teachers,

Different faces and different bullies.

Fresh new pair of books to read and failed attempts at friends.

The only thing that remained stable was my grades which made me a prodigy.

If that didn't speak volumes, then I don't know what else does.

At some point, I just gave up,

Built-up walls with the pages of books,

So I wouldn't be disappointed by my social expectations.

Defective Dandelions

I used to love

Dandelions.

I would make a wish each time

I found one.

I stopped when I realized

They wouldn't come true.

How the game goes

When you play tag,

You run from the person who is "it".

The thing is,

She was always "it"

Outside of the game.

Running till her lungs gave out,

In search of someone.

                              But they all have run away.

Diana the Bear

Diana,

That was her name.

She wore a pink sweater with a logo.

I'm the beginning she was an unclaimed bear.

Standing there for a potential owner.

Her eyes stared into mine.

"That one," I said.

Maybe it was my imagination,

But the corner of Diana's mouth went up.

Finally,

Diana had a home.

Learn To Be Nice

Kids can be mean,

Some are because they do not know the extent of their words.

Saying them without ramifications.

Learning what is right and wrong can be so important.

But as one ages,

A person begins to realize,

Maybe,

If he, she, or they, knew

The fragility of the human race,

Maybe,

Just maybe,

There would be fewer arguments,

Maltreatment,

And possibly a better sense of

Peace.

Prices of Magic and Monsters

Growing up is realizing

Why fairies stay hidden.

They stare in horror

As phone cameras expose them with their bright flashes.

Violating their peace.

It's no wonder vampires are gone.

That price is living for eternity is full of loneliness.

Watching loved ones come and go.

It's unfathomable.

One who has felt loss,

Can understand

The feeling of walking

With half a heart.

Or in this case,

Walking in a soulless corpse.

The Unthinkable

I miss the toys,

The joy of watching cartoons on the weekends,

And

When all it took was singing lullabies to myself to
help me sleep,

Instead of medicine.

I miss the simple times.

Do you have Change?

Why do **I** have to pay the price

For something *they* did?

A Poem from my Younger self

I'm trapped in a cage that I can't escape.

They say their doing this for my own good, but are
they?

From time to time I see people pass by.

Some ignore me while others don't.

No one has tried to break the lock.

They're too busy with theirs to try.

In my cage, I block out every sound.

Especially the screams and shouts.

If I'm ever free from this, they'd put me on a leash.

I only have but one trusted companion to talk to.

He is the only one who ever listens.

With all the pain I have carried he helps me release

it.

No matter how many times I thrash and scream

I know that I won't be free.

But I know one day it will happen.

Until then I shall continue to wait

Even if there is a price I must pay.

My Choice

I know they wanted a doctor.

You wanted to be one so badly.

But as we got older,

We realize that being a doctor wasn't our dream.

You may not understand,

As a child,

But now we know,

What our hearts wanted.

They Got to Me

What I find sad

Is that when someone calls us

beautiful,

You would've believed it.

But I,

Now older,

I am unsure if that is true.

Little Knight

One thing,

I admire about you,

Little one,

Is

How brave you were.

It was you who fought them,

So that your younger siblings didn't have to.

That took guts for a little girl.

Unphased

You were never afraid to get your hands dirty.

That may be because,

Not even the dirt could stain your

Limits.

Never one to be selfish

For every candle, you blew,

Your wish was never for you.

Every dessert was shared

At the table

When there was none left.

You gave them your dignity at the expense of their
smile.

A Solo Lap

The sun against my skin

Burned,

But the wind made up for it.

My hair flew in the air behind me.

My glasses dirty from the precipitation

Of my sweat.

Still, I continued to run from it all

On the track of the playground.

Brushed by shock

To that kid who punched my stomach,

As I was hanging from the monkey bars,

And caused me to fall into a sensation of

a heart aching chest pain,

and sudden immobility,

I hope you fall off your bike and broke a bone like
how I almost have.

What am I?

Don't let the pigment of my skin fool you.

My tongue can speak volumes of dialogues in Spanish,

As it was my first language,

Yet

I still couldn't fit in

Either way.

Snow Day

The first time I saw snow falling from the sky,

I had thought it was pixie dust.

It looked so beautiful

And made drinking hot chocolate taste even better.

I put on my barbie gloves

And a pink beanie.

Within seconds I was out the door making snow angels

And having snowball fights.

I would stick my tongue out to see

How it tasted and be surprised as it faded.

The lightness of it made me believe that maybe,

Just maybe there had been pixie dust.

Because all it took was pieces of ice from the sky,

To create one of my fondest memories.

This was one of the good days.

Ladylike

I wasn't always fond of dresses.

It would always upset me

Because with a dress,

I could not run,

I could not jump,

I could not play.

It would not be proper to do so with a dress.

But I didn't care.

Too Young for This

Pt.2

I wish they didn't talk about my body.

In the Books

I was always one to live in

My mind,

And in world

Where I could feel like a badass with a sword.

What they See

You would be surprised

At how much I have

Broken the mirror

That held the perfections on the surface of the reflection.

Because I was a girl

Here are thing things I wasn't allowed to do:

- Discuss and expose the patriarchy
- Use my voice
- Run in a dress
- Play sports with the boys
- Play with toy cars
- Wear certain clothes
- Cut my hair short
- Trade for something more "masculine"
- Pick the color blue, even though it was my favorite color
- Make decisions of my own

What to Learn

They should've taught me how to stand up for myself, instead of teaching me how to:

Behave,

Act,

And dress.

What is family

Over the years,

Family

Was no longer about blood.

You would laugh and ask, "What do you mean ?"

Anyone would find it silly, but it was far from that.

Sometimes blood can only go so far

Some blood can turn rotten somehow or even

Turn yours cold.

People who we once called strangers,

Lifted you,

Supported you,

And did more than what those of blood could.

Now, I will not say that all of those with our blood are bad,

But

Those who go beyond blood provided you with much more than basic needs.

"Family is what you create together, not what is in your DNA" would be my final response.

Past, Present, and Future

There are various things that

I regret

Whether it is what we did and/or didn't do.

I could list them out but there is no point,

Since there is no turning back the clock.

Yet,

I cannot keep walking away from it all,

For now, I must deal with the consequences.

In hopes that our future self,

Can finally move on once and for all.

Free from these strings I am cutting one at a time.

You, the victim.

I, the healer,

And she, the survivor.

Eyes Don't Lie

Don't let these round glasses fool you,

They've seen things that

No child should see.

They carried the blueprints

And memorized each word that has been written.

Her quiet nature is what

Let her be a fly on the wall

And a mouse underneath your feet.

Though, she would never dare to strike like a snake.

Because that is not what she is.

All she does is sees with those round glasses.

She sees things

More than you will

Ever know.

Behind the Curtain

Oh, honey,

You can keep the dolls fooled for so long,

Before they end up finding out

Who you really are

Behind the dollhouse.

Brainwashed

She always wondered why she didn't look like them.

Why she didn't have those eyes,

That nose, that hair,

Everything that they had that she wasn't

Complimented for.

She wanted the life she saw on the TV.

Their clothes,

Phones,

And

Style,

Yet she didn't have a cent to spare for any of those.

They knew how badly she wanted it all.

Of course, they did.

They were the ones who put those thoughts in her head.

They knew what they were doing.

Let Us Be

One of my greatest accomplishments is learning to

Listen to the beat of my own drum.

Instead of their ridiculous comments.

In doing so I found great independence

And

Confidence in my actions.

I no longer am ashamed of what brings me joy.

I know that I will always be a clown in their eyes
for not being like *them*.

But at least,

I am free.

I will not laugh at other people for what they like,

Nor will I ever be the reason someone stops smiling.

Just like you, I refuse to go by the picture-perfect guidelines of society.

If that is what makes me a clown.

Then I guess, I'll go ahead and create my own circus.

Overworked

Pages were scattered everywhere

Most if not burned,

Were eventually torn.

The ink from the pen trickled crimson.

It laid there lifeless.

"Don't worry, it's just sleeping."

It needed just one more page,

To be enough.

"Come on now."

Their Point of View

Of course, they hate her.

Look at her,

The attention she gets.

It's not fair that she got an award.

She did nothing.

I bet she doesn't have to lift a finger.

Let's beat her up.

Show her who is on top.

Why are you using smart words?

Am I too stupid for you?

You're trying too hard.

Why is she wearing that?

You would look better without the glasses.

Little did they know,

I only did what I was told.

I did not mean any harm,

Or to feed into their envy.

I guess that's the consequence of a prodigy.

Her Own Game

Between all the

X's and O's

In tic-tac-toe

Were lines

Of

Boundaries

of her and

Them.

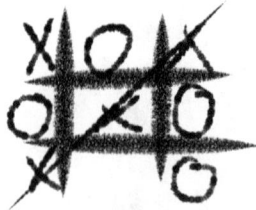

Unveiling Beneath the Facade

Among these poems,

You may think that I was merely weak,

That I complain too much,

Or I have been overdramatic.

It was quite the opposite.

I drowned myself with false happiness

And went along with everything.

I was submissive and silent.

Realistically,

That is how I coped with it all.

Because who would want a sad child?

So you see,

This is why I am so loud now.

I am processing it all

At once.

Now I am aware of the real damage.

And even if no one reads this,

Speaking my truth is

What is healing me.

Blind sighted

The number of red flags

Never compared to the different colors

Of their heart.

It wasn't that they were born this way,

But rather they became tainted.

Dance

She didn't know the song

Nor how to follow the steps,

But that did not

Take away from the

Twirls and lightness of her hair against the dancefloor.

She wasn't dancing with a ghost.

She was dancing with a soul.

Entities not Wanted

There it was,

planet earth.

The alien looked out the window gleefully

Excited about the new species.

Surely, they are just like our kind

With the exception of a different galaxy.

Little did the alien know,

That these species do not lead with their heart as
they do on their planet,

These species

lead with their fists.

So when the spaceship landed on a grassland,

Instead of being met with greetings,

The alien had been bombarded with bullets.

What could the alien have done?

Did they do something to initiate war?

Was their ship too bright?

The alien became afraid.

Shouts ruptured and flames caught the ship.

No hugs or cuddles can solve this like on the alien's planet.

These species were far too barbaric.

The alien didn't like the planet anymore.

Glamour

Under all those accessories

Was

A

Cracked mirror,

And

A frightened

Creature.

The Shadow Lady

The best part about hiding in broad daylight

Is that they will never suspect a thing.

I grow an inch

Minute by minute

Until I eventually consume you.

I don't go after just anyone.

I have standards.

With that being said, you'll never guess who is next.

~~You, my darling.~~

~~See you soon....~~

Special Little Gem

I glow and glimmer.

You need me in the night, don't you?

I come with a cost.

You cannot take me off,

Nor would you want to.

I bring great strength

And

Powers beyond belief.

That is if you believe.

It's the only way I'll work.

If Truth Was a Man

"Oh honey" he snickered with his hand lightly
touching my chin.

"For someone so smart, you're pretty stupid."

He laughed at his remark.

"Come, don't cry.

You knew this was going to happen

Didn't you?"

Bliss of the Story Told

The only way

She was able to rationalize

Every bad thing that happened to her

Was

Convincing herself

That she was the main character.

All bad things happen to the main character, right?

So she must be on the right track to becoming

Something more.

Little did she know,

Not all main characters have happy endings...

154

Rumor Has it

It didn't matter if what they said was

True or not.

What mattered to her

Was if they believed it.

Imaginary friends

There is a legend my uncle told me,

That all imaginary friends weren't

Necessarily imaginary,

But rather the souls of those who

Died as a child.

It's no wonder why I had so many,

And why

All they wanted to do was play.

Coming Clean too Late

For years I didn't tell my parents

About the bullies,

The bruises,

And why I wanted to switch schools.

They had too much to worry about.

I didn't want to add to the pile.

They had my brother,

And my newborn baby sister.

It wasn't until years later,

When I finally felt safe at a school

And stable at home,

Was when I told them everything.

The details spilled like a pipe that has burst.

The thing is,

it didn't matter anymore

Because there was nothing they can do,

It already happened

And I was no longer dealing with these problems,

Just only their effects.

Preventing it

I think part of her didn't want revenge,

She wanted to be recognized.

She wanted them to understand the effects of their actions,

So that they don't do that to anyone else.

Unlikely Friends

They never got along.

He would always pick the scabs on his hands,

And she would squirm each time.

They would always argue.

They shared several glares

And

hated how they were always assigned as partners
for every other group assignment.

But just like her,

He too was picked on,

Shared the same nickname of "four-eyes"

And she felt sympathy every time the others made
him cry or feel scared

Because she too knew what it felt like.

~

One day the little girl stumbled upon him crying.

She had a stuffed tiger

That she got from the principal office.

Feeling bad, she shared her tiger.

For a while, they passed it back and forth

Like an unspoken agreement.

In the end, he had the tiger.

Before he could return it,

She was gone.

Because she had moved,

She never saw him

Or the tiger again.

She hoped that at least

The tiger will suffice for her absence.

Scared Little Girl

They all thought she was insane.

She kept talking to herself,

Trembling at the slightest flashes of light,

And often wept at times without explanation.

Maybe if they asked,

They would notice demons in her head.

Lost in Labels

She spent nights studying

Relentlessly

Because

"Being smart" was the only thing she can prove she
was good at.

That was her role

And what she thought was her purpose.,

She had to keep that role.

No matter what.

A's were all she needed instead of air to catch her
breath

While she was lost

In the jungle

Of

Those demands.

Do What you Love Before it's Too Late

She loved to sing,

Oh, she could sing for hours!

It's such a shame

That she has lost her voice

That was locked in a box,

And traded it for

An instrument she can barely play.

What a sad woman with an instrument she became.

Playtime is Over

What hurt

Was finding out that

No matter how much I changed myself,

And followed their rules,

I was never fun enough to play with them.

That's when I started to

Unveil my true self since there was no more reason

To play pretend anymore.

Beware of the Girl

If we were a warning label it would be:

> *Caution, world's greatest*
>
> *decipher and deceiver*

'Selfish'

She didn't want kids,

It wasn't because she was being selfish.

More so,

She spent most of her life

With the experience of taking care of them.

She lost her childhood

And wasn't willing to

Trade her adulthood

At that rate.

It's her turn now.

If that is what made her selfish,

Then they are the ones who should be claimed as cruel

To even demand such a thing

Knowing its price.

Sudden Shifts

It's quite laughable

Of how many more

Plot twists there are in our lives,

Then those in murder mysteries we've read.

Passed Down Lessons

She hated that she was always seen as the bad guy,

When all she ever did for them,

Was stop them from

Making the same

Mistakes she did.

Big Sister Syndrome

They all came to her when they needed something.

Even when she was busy,

She had to make room.

When she was present,

It felt like walking in eggs shells.

She knew that whatever she did they did too.

She was constantly torn

Of the role.

All she wanted to be was a sister.

Their dependency on her

Was a heavy one.

When she wasn't needed,

And she had time for herself,

She then returned to her own battles,

Because no one is old enough to help her fight them.

Amnesty

There are multiple people,

I still cannot forgive,

And forget to this day.

Some being the people who I use to call

family.

One-Sided Exchange

It wasn't until they grew up,

And didn't need her,

That she understood

she traded half of her life,

For theirs.

Maybe in Another Life

It always crosses my mind,

Of how different I would be,

If the world was a bit nicer,

And the only person I needed to worry about

Was me.

That's How it All Came

Crashing Down

Too many times,

You had gone

Into your room

To feel what you had suppressed

And

Read out your feelings through the eyes of fictional
characters.

Too many times

you had been let down

By pretty lies that glimmered

Behind fake plastic gems.

Too many times

You were told to hold it in,

Because there was no room for

Your feelings.

Yet,

Only once,

You were able to find

Someone who gave you a reason to smile

Every single day.

But that was lost,

When he died.

Her Own Master

The day she realized

That no one

Would help,

Was the day

She learned to

Teach

Herself.

Born to Lead

You are all fools,

No ragged clothes,

Torn shoes,

And belittlement,

Would stop a princess from being a queen.

Don't Let You Limits Shape You, Shape those Limits Instead

She didn't have much.

She has a big log,

And a small knife.

With that small

Knife,

Rather than use it to steal,

Or

Kill,

She carved out a sword,

And became the best warrior there was.

Best yet,

She still kept that little knife

To remind her

To be the odds

When it was against her.

I Found You

You were there on the floor crying.

You were shaking and completely cold and scared.

I barely recognized you.

I wanted to cry.

When I reach for your hand,

They were cold.

A tear fell from my eyes, and you wiped it off my cheek,

When I should've been the one to do that for you a long time ago.

I found you

And will never let you.

Reunited

After all these years,

I kept our favorite plushies safe,

Because I knew someday

We'd meet again,

And that you would need them.

Regrets

I wished I never hated the smile we

Had,

Because it was absolutely beautiful.

For the longest time,

I avoided mirrors,

Photos,

And anything that showed our face

Because I hated how we looked that much.

I wish we didn't hate that,

Because now I'm obsessed

With our glow.

I hated the way we laugh and talked.

So I kept quiet and hid in the background.

I don't hate that anymore.

Because all of this is just being human.

I wish I hadn't hated myself this much.

I deeply regret spending so many years wasted on
what others have been shoving down our throats.

When we should've spent it loving it as I do now.

Inner Child's Perspective

While I didn't like the things you did,

Especially with me out of the picture,

I knew why you did it.

Because you did what you had to do,

To keep us safe

At the expense of ruining the fake person we built.

And that is why I'll never hold it against you.

My Perspective

If am being honest,

Part of me feared talking to you because I thought
you'd hate me

Like how I once hated you.

But you never did.

All you ever wanted was to love and to

Be loved.

You smiled at me and said,

"Don't worry older me, I forgive you."

With the softest hug, I haven't had in years.

A wave of relief hit me...

And just like that, I was the one crying into your arms instead.

Climb your Plane

When I was little,

There was a park with an enormous fake plane.

Every kid would climb the plane

And the brave ones would make it up to the wings.

Bit by bit I climbed my way up to the wings

But I was always too scared to make it to the top.

I was scared of falling up from the wings.

One day my father challenged me to make it to the top.

I took the challenge and tried.

I was very close,

So close but I turned around.

"Why did you stop?" He would ask.

"You could've made it." He then further encouraged
me to make it.

Being a daddy's girl,

I listened and made it to the wings.

I clung so hard to make sure I wouldn't fall.

It felt windy up here, but the view was absolutely
stuffing.

The chills in my body felt nice.

Exhilarating even.

I looked down and saw my father smiling.

Like always,

He always knew I had it in me.

On the drive back,

I learned a lesson that day.

"Never let fear prevent you

From reaching your goals." My father said.

Child at Heart

Deep down

We're all kids in

Adult bodies.

My Response to My Younger Self.

I am here to tell you

That we made our way out of the cage.

The boy you imagined was a fake hero we created

But he was just enough to keep us sane.

We can't fly yet but with your help

I am sure we can make ourselves

A pair of wings.

You are probably wondering

How we did.

You may not like it,

But for us to break free

The cost was cutting ties with people you've always thought we'd keep close.

And for me to become a cold-hearted monster.

Overcomers

I'm glad

We aren't scared of

Them anymore,

At least not like we use to.

You Saved Me

I'm glad I didn't

Give up on

~~Us~~

You.

I'm glad you didn't give up too.

-I.C

If I Could Tell Her

If I could turn back time,

I would tell her

To Glow like a fairy,

To Be the child she was.

I would tell her

Not to worry so much.

Not to care,

And to do more with her time,

Then wasting it on grades that

Didn't measure her intelligence.

I would tell her

To not hate herself.

Because she was not like everyone else.

I would tell her that

That was my favorite part about us.

I would tell her so many things,

Especially the ones that we'd always wish

Someone other than ourselves would've told us.

Let's Have a Seat

Now that we're free,

And I have found you,

There are many things we need to learn.

I will need your help to find that child-like joy,

And you'll need lessons from me about

Strength.

There is a lot more to say but that is for another day.

I hope now, we can find a new start

But of course before we start anew, we must discuss

the

Big bad

Wolf that is our past.

Sincerely Older me,

I don't hate you like I used to.

I used to think we were two completely different
persons,

Yet you were still battling the same insecurities that
I am fighting now.

Only, that I chose to forget that

Until now.

Now I looked at our photos, I want to hug you each
and every time.

And stared in horror at what we became to
ourselves.

I became like the people we'd said we never would

I am so sorry for hating you,

When I should've

Been the one lifting you up.

Now I will embrace you.

Every single part.

Even if others will ridicule me,

I'll finally let us live.

Most important of all,

I'll give you the love and acceptance we deserved.

I'll protect you.

No more damages

And hatred towards you.

I'll never do that to you again,

I promise.

P.S

Although I don't say this much,

I love you,

-Alexa.

CPSIA information can be obtained
at www.ICGtesting.com
Printed in the USA
BVHW062025160123
656382BV00015B/743

9 781088 063903